Children of the World

Sweden

For their help in the preparation of *Children of the World: Sweden*, the editors gratefully thank Claes Åkerblom, Bo-Gunnar Gustavsson, Darcie Gustavsson, and Lillian Larson, Milwaukee, Wis.; the Embassy of Sweden (U.S.), Washington, D.C.; the Embassy of Sweden (Canada), Ottawa; the International Institute, Milwaukee; the Swedish Institute, Stockholm, Sweden; Rachel Oestreicher Haspel and the Raoul Wallenberg Committee of the United States, New York City; and the Swedish Vasa Order of America.

For Raoul Wallenberg

Library of Congress Cataloging-in-Publication Data

Bjener, Tamiko.
  Sweden.

  (Children of the world)
  Bibliography: p.
  Includes index.
  Summary: Text and photographs present life in Sweden
by following eleven-year-old Isabel, child of divorced
parents, as she moves between her two families.
  1. Sweden — Social life and customs — Juvenile
literature. 2. Children — Sweden — Juvenile literature.
3. Lapps — Sweden — Juvenile literature. [1. Sweden.
2. Family life — Sweden] I. Knowlton, MaryLee, 1946-
II. Sachner, Mark, 1948- . III. Series: Children
of the world (Milwaukee, Wis.)
DL631.B475   1987   948.5   86-42803
ISBN 1-55532-189-5
ISBN 1-55532-164-X (lib. bdg.)

North American edition first published in 1987 by

Gareth Stevens, Inc.
7317 West Green Tree Road   Milwaukee, Wisconsin 53223, USA

This work was originally published in shortened form consisting of section I only.
Photographs and original text copyright © 1986 by Tamiko Bjener.
Photography on page 50 by Eivon Carlson, courtesy of the Swedish Institute of Stockholm.
First and originally published by Kaisei-sha Publishing Co., Ltd., Tokyo.
World English rights arranged with Kaisei-sha Publishing Co., Ltd. through
Japan Foreign-Rights Centre.

Typeset by Ries Graphics ltd., Milwaukee.
Design: Laurie Shock.
Map design: Gary Moseley.

3 4 5 6 7 8 9 92 91 90 89 88

Children of the World

Sweden

Photography
by Tamiko Bjener

Edited by
MaryLee Knowlton &
Mark J. Sachner

Gareth Stevens Publishing
Milwaukee

. . . a note about *Children of the World*:

The children of the world live in fishing towns and urban centers, on islands and in mountain valleys, on sheep ranches and fruit farms. This series follows one child in each country through the pattern of his or her life. Candid photographs show the children with their families, at school, at play, and in their communities. The text describes the dreams of the children and, often through their own words, tells how they see themselves and their lives.

Each book also explores events that are unique to the country in which the child lives, including festivals, religious ceremonies, and national holidays. The *Children of the World* series does more than tell about foreign countries. It introduces the children of each country and shows readers what it is like to be a child in that country.

. . . and about *Sweden*:

Isabel's parents are divorced so, like many North American children, she has two families. She is an important member of both families. Although she is only 11, Isabel already has opinions about many social and international issues. But like kids everywhere, Isabel doesn't let the serious side of her life keep her from having fun times with her friends.

To enhance this book's value in libraries and classrooms, comprehensive reference sections include up-to-date data about Sweden's geography, demographics, language, currency, education, culture, industry, and natural resources. *Sweden* also features a bibliography, research topics, activity projects, and discussions of such subjects as Stockholm, the country's history, political system, ethnic and religious composition, and language.

The living conditions and experiences of children in Sweden vary according to economic, environmental, and ethnic circumstances. The reference sections help bring to life for young readers the diversity and richness of the culture and heritage of Sweden. Of particular interest are discussions of the Lapps, or Sami, a native culture that has made its presence felt in the language and tradition of Sweden.

CONTENTS

Isabel and her mother, Marthe, with their dog Linus.

LIVING IN SWEDEN:
Isabel, a Girl with Two Families

Isabel Eggers is 11 years old. She lives in the suburbs of Stockholm, the capital of Sweden. Her home is in the Tensta Apartment Complex. It is a 20-minute subway ride from Stockholm's Central Station. She lives with her mother and a dog named Linus in a two-bedroom apartment on the fourth floor. On the door are two names, Eggers and Bergland.

Isabel and Linus outside her apartment complex.

Hej, jag heter Isabel Eggers

"Hello, my name is Isabel Eggers!"

Isabel with her father and his new family: Kii, Olivia, Isabel, and Jens.

Isabel's parents were divorced when she was a baby. She has kept her father's last name. During the week, Isabel lives with her mother. But she stays with her father every other weekend, five weeks in the summer, and every other Christmas holiday. Isabel's parents are friendly even though they are divorced. Sometimes Isabel and her mother join her father's new family for dinner or a movie.

Isabel and her mother have breakfast together. Soon they will be off to school and work.

In Sweden, many children's parents are divorced. However, both parents must raise and educate their children. Therefore, ties between the children and the parents stay strong. The question of where the children will live is very important. If they are old enough, the children may help make the decision. Till she was five, Isabel spent one week with her father and the next with her mother. When she started school, Isabel and her parents decided on the plan they have now.

A winter play area at Isabel's apartment block.

A summer play area.

Apartment complexes in Sweden are planned for families with children. They usually have playgrounds for summer and winter sports. There may be play areas inside as well.

Marthe's work place at the University of Stockholm: the Geographical Research Institute.

Marthe's Job

Isabel's mother's name is Marthe Bergland. She is a laboratory technician at the University of Stockholm. She works only part-time so she can spend time with Isabel.

Today Isabel has dropped by her mother's office. Children in Sweden often visit their parents at their work place. Teachers in Sweden believe children should learn about their parents' jobs.

Isabel's desk.

Isabel prepares her own dinner.

Isabel and Marthe's kitchen.

Twice a week Isabel's mother has a chemistry class. On these nights Isabel makes her own dinner. Her mother has taught her to mix spaghetti with tomato sauce, top it with a sprinkle of cheese, and bake it in the oven. When her mother gets home they talk about the day and make plans for tomorrow. Tonight they talk about the dog, who hasn't seemed well lately. They decide to take him to the vet after school and work.

Reading and talking before bed.

Isabel takes the subway to her father's apartment
in central Stockholm.

Isabel and her six-year-old half sister, Olivia.

At Home with Jens, Kii, and Olivia

This Friday, Isabel is going to her father's home after
school. Her father, Jens Eggers, lives in an elegant
building built in the early 1900s. On his door is a sign
which reads "Non-Nuclear Zone." Like many Swedes,
Jens and his wife, Kii, are members of the anti-
nuclear movement. Isabel, too, worries about
nuclear weapons destroying the world. Swedish
parents raise their children to be aware of issues that
affect them. They are encouraged to have opinions.

Jens' apartment building.

Jens is a radio newscaster. Isabel listens to him in the
morning before school. Kii is a nurse.
Jens and Kii have a daughter,
Isabel's half sister, Olivia.

An underground art gallery in the subway near Jens' apartme

The street where Jens, Kii, and Olivia live.

Saturday breakfast, 9 a.m. It's still dark, and everyone's half asleep!

Winter breakfasts bring everyone to the table in the dark. It will stay dark most of the morning and be dark again by early afternoon. The light from the Advent candles lifts everyone's spirits. But it takes a real effort to stay cheerful.

After breakfast, Jens gives Isabel 11 krona of weekend pocket money. She goes off to find her "Saturday treat." She sometimes tries to save up pocket money from her father. But usually she spends it on candy. Her favorite is *saltlakrits*, a licorice candy with a slightly salty taste.

Isabel and her father prepare lunch.

Isabel chooses her "Saturday treat."

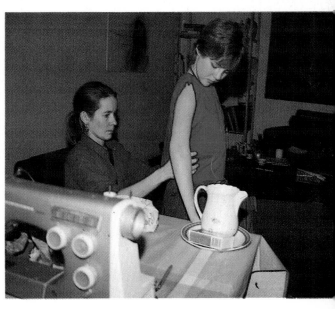

Kii makes a dress for Isabel.

Isabel and Kii spend Saturday afternoon making a dress for Isabel. She will wear it to parties during the holiday season. Late in the afternoon, Isabel makes boiled potatoes. They go well with a Swedish meal of herring, salad, and lingonberries.

Isabel and Olivia enjoy being sisters.

Olivia's desk.

Isabel and her sister, Olivia, have only lived together for short visits at a time. Still, they are very close. They share a bedroom, and Isabel comforts Olivia when she has nightmares. Isabel is not so happy listening to Olivia's snoring. But she likes being an older sister.

Isabel clowns around in Kii's high heels.

Isabel and Marisa are old friends who enjoy a good talk and a good laugh.

Isabel and Marisa — Good Friends

Isabel and Marisa are longtime good friends. When they were little, they played together and shared toys. Now they share secrets and dreams. Marisa's parents are also divorced, though more recently. She remembers living with them when they were not getting along. It is easier to see them apart and happy.

Like boys, girls want careers when they grow up. Marisa and Isabel are thinking already about what they want to do. In a few years they will choose programs in high school that will lead to a career. Isabel thinks about working among Sweden's growing immigrant population. Many programs help immigrants adjust to their new lives. Isabel wants to work for one of these programs.

Taking the train to Uncle Per's country house. With any luck, they'll have their cozy compartment all to themselves for the whole trip.

Summer in Sweden

Swedes make the most of the long, light days of summer. Sweden is quite far north. In fact, part of it is inside the Arctic Circle. Its winter is therefore long and its summer short. The high latitude also affects the light. In winter there are days in northern Sweden without any light at all. And during June and July, northern Sweden has its "white nights" when the sun never sets.

School closes for summer in mid June. Swedish workers have five weeks of vacation a year, and many people take off when their children are out of school. Many city people go to summer homes in the country. Or they travel. They may camp or stay in hostels throughout Sweden. Summer is the time to be outdoors.

Isabel, her mother, and Marisa travel by train to visit her Uncle Per. He has a country house up north in Sundsvall. Uncle Per meets them at the train station. He is Marthe's brother. The two of them have spent their summers here since they were children with their parents. When they were little, Marthe and Per used to carry milk in buckets every morning from the neighbors' farm.

Isabel, Marthe, and Marisa travel with Linus on the train.

The sea is right in front of Uncle Per's house.

A restful moment in the house.

Sundsvall is about 155 miles (250 km) north of Stockholm. It is on the sea, on the Gulf of Bothnia. In the morning, Isabel and Marisa are up early. They race to the beach. They love the feel of the cool sand in the morning.

Isabel has thought often of the beach through the long winter. She loves to run along the edge of the water and play tag with the cold water. By late afternoon she is refreshed and tired at the same time.

24

Isabel samples a blueberry. She finds them everywhere she looks.

Mountain
lingonberries.

Late in the day, Isabel goes for a long walk in the woods. The lingonberries she finds will make a delicious dessert for dinner. Her mother will mix them gently with sugar and beaten egg whites. They will make a dish that some people call the pink cloud. The forest is full of other wild berries — raspberries, strawberries, blueberries, and cloudberries.

A fine crop of mushrooms.

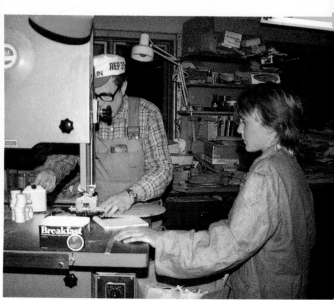

It's summer's end, and Isabel buys wooden crafts for souvenirs.

The second Wednesday in August is the opening of the crayfish season. It is early in the day. Uncle Per takes Isabel to his secret place for mushroom hunting. At the foot of a cedar tree they find a bed of yellow mushrooms hidden under the grass. This year's heavy rains have resulted in a bumper crop of mushrooms. Isabel's basket is soon full.

Dinner is loud and merry. Neighbors are invited to share the feast of wild mushrooms in cream sauce, bread and cheese, and, of course, crayfish. They all wear funny hats and bibs. They forget about table manners as they try to get every last bit of crayfish out of the shell. Everyone knows the summer is almost over.

Isabel chops the mushrooms.
They will be fried and cooked in a cream sauce. Everyone will shell the boiled crayfish at the table.

Isabel's school, the Elinsborg School.

Isabel and Her Friends at School

Vacation is over. Isabel has the same teacher and classmates she had last year. This helps her adjust quickly to the new school year. Mrs. Esbensen starts the day by reading aloud to help them settle down. This morning the book is about a boy who has migrated to Sweden from Finland. When she finishes the story, Mrs. Esbensen asks the students to tell about the books they read over the summer. Swedish children all learn English in school, and Isabel happily tells the class about a book she read from the United States — *The Beast in the Bathtub*, by Kathleen Stevens.

The subway station in Tensta has a beautiful mural in it. The mural has an inscription which reads, "The rest of the world has come to Sweden, and contact with immigrants has enriched our life and culture." Many people have migrated to Sweden as workers, political refugees, and poor people with no country to call home.

The Tensta Apartment Complex has new Swedes from Turkey, Greece, and Finland. Isabel's school has many children from these families. Her fifth grade class is small, with only 12 students; so her teacher can give special instruction to children who cannot speak Swedish well yet.

Isabel and Marisa peek out of their classroom.

Mrs. Esbensen and her class.

Isabel listens during class discussion.

Mrs. Esbensen helps each student with her or his math.

Math and Swedish are required of everybody. The students study their math by themselves. They read the textbook and solve the problems at their own pace. Mrs. Esbensen does not work at the blackboard. Instead, she comes to each student's desk and works with that student alone.

The teachers' room is a busy place!

Isabel's desk.

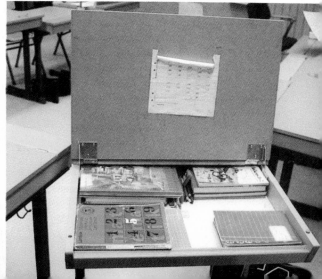

Isabel likes taking part in class discussions.

Current events.

Isabel's drawing of Dandy, her dream horse.

The students learn Swedish in groups. They read from many sources, including newspapers. Some of the textbooks are filled with illustrations, and Mrs. Esbensen encourages the children to discuss the stories they are reading.

Isabel's language group.

A Swedish language textbook.

The cafeteria at lunchtime.

Isabel finishes her pannbiff.

The class has a meeting once a month. They choose who
will represent the class for the month at school meetings and
programs. Today Marisa was elected class head. The students
also set some class rules: not to make noise in the classroom;
not to lean too far back in the desk chairs; to hang one's jacket
properly; not to scribble graffiti; and not to bring candy to
school. Everyone agreed on most of the rules. But the candy rule
passed by a narrow margin!

Children eat lunch in a bright dining room with their teacher. Today the menu includes *pannbiff*. Pannbiff is a kind of hamburger. It is eaten with cranberry relish, potatoes, salad, hard bread, and milk. Often the meals include food introduced to Sweden by its recent immigrants. Even at meals the children learn what all of Sweden's cultures have to offer. The school's 260 students eat in two shifts. The dining room bustles with their cheer.

After lunch the children play outside, whatever the weather. The fresh air helps them feel energetic and alert for their afternoon classes. Often they will play a pickup game of soccer, but today the girls play ball by themselves.

The playground at lunchtime.

Playground hockey.

This afternoon is free for non-required courses. Students can choose what they like from swimming, hockey, ping-pong, bread-making, stamp-collecting, and gymnastics. Last term, Isabel took hockey. This term, she is taking gymnastics. Next term, Isabel plans to take swimming. She likes the more active electives.

Gymnastics.

Classes are over, and everyone heads home.

Horseriding after school.

School's Out!

After school Isabel and Marisa must take Linus for his daily walk. Afterwards, they have a couple of hours free. Marisa suggests that they call up people and pretend to be someone else. But Isabel has a better idea. "Let's go see Hedvig!" she suggests. Hedvig is Marisa's horse, which she keeps on a farm.

The girls prepare snacks of bread and cheese and fill a thermos with juice. After walking 10 minutes from their bus stop, they can smell the horses. Hedvig is munching grass, and Marisa runs off to stroke his head. Isabel is taking riding lessons and hopes someday to have a horse of her own. Two hours flash by quickly.

37

St. Lucia's Day

December 13th is St. Lucia's Day, the beginning of the Christmas season. Lucia was an Italian girl. She became a saint after she was burned to death for her Christian faith 1600 years ago. As St. Lucia's Day approaches the days become shorter and darker. Even in Stockholm, which is in the south of Sweden, it gets light at only ten or eleven in the morning. By two in the afternoon, it is already dark.

In the dark days before St. Lucia's Day, you can smell the bread and cookies baking in ovens. They smell delicious as their aroma fills the streets! In both of her parents' apartments, Isabel is busy with the baking and decorating that are part of this happy season.

Isabel's mother and Kii make gingerbread.

Making marzipan out of crushed almonds.

Marzipan: Art you can eat, by Isabel and Marthe!

Long before dawn on December 13th, a yearly custom is about to take place in families all over Sweden. The oldest daughter — or a "borrowed" daughter — is awake. She dresses as St. Lucia in a long white gown with a red sash and a crown of candles. The red sash symbolizes the martyr's blood of St. Lucia. Younger sisters come along as maids. Boys called starboys wear cone-shaped paper hats with stars on them. "St. Lucia" carries a tray with coffee, saffron bread, and ginger cookies into her parents' bedroom. As they enter, all the children sing St. Lucia carols. Throughout the day the ceremony is repeated in offices and schools.

Isabel usually waits for her mother to wake her in the morning. Today, however, she set her alarm herself. She dresses in her costume and assembles the traditional treats on her tray. Then she goes in to wake her mother. It's very early, but Isabel is too excited to go back to sleep. Today is the beginning of the Christmas season, a time of festivities and good will.

It's early in the morning on St. Lucia's Day.

Isabel and Marthe celebrate the beginning of the holiday season.

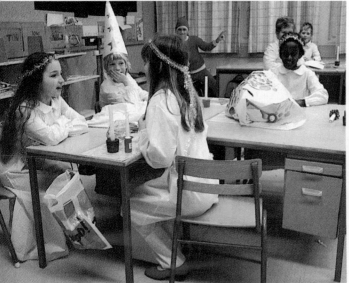

Waiting for the curtain to rise on the St. Lucia play.

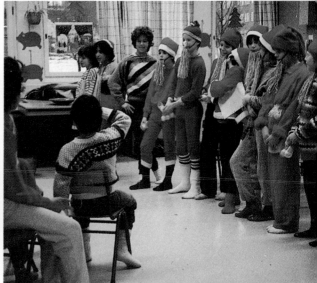

Isabel's class performs a play about Santa Claus, who is also called jultomte.

The children sing carols by candlelight.

Christmastime

December 21 is the last day of the term. All the students gather in the gymnasium for the school's Christmas party. The younger children hold candles and sing carols. Isabel's class presents a funny Christmas play they have written to entertain the other classes. The principal wishes peace and freedom in the new year for all children everywhere.

"See you after the holidays!"

The children leave school in high spirits. The term is over. Mrs. Esbensen has told Isabel's mother that she has done well in all her studies. Isabel is pleased. Her mother thinks she can do even better, though. But that's a matter for next term. Now it's time for Christmas.

A huge Christmas reindeer display.

Christmas decorations sold at the florist's shop.

Work and school have kept Isabel and Marthe busy. Now they must get started with their shopping. Isabel makes a long list of what she wants for Christmas. She figures this should make things easier for her mother! At the top of the list is a horse. She knows, however, that a horse is not likely this year. More likely are other things on her list — a game, a T-shirt dress, earrings, silver bracelets, stockings, make-up, jeans, and smelly erasers. Isabel has another list — of gifts she wants to buy for her friends and families. She already has things in mind for her mother and Olivia. But the others will take some looking around.

Holiday decorations light up a plaza in downtown Stockholm. In addition to shops, this plaza has a library and a children's craft center.

Holiday fun: Ice skating in Stockholm.

Isabel and her mother have bought a tree. They found it in a lot near the subway station. On Christmas Eve they put it up. The whole apartment glows with its soft candle light. The tree will stay up till Knut's Day in mid January. Knut's Day marks the end of the Christmas season. It is the excuse for one last party. Friends gather to help take down the tree and to eat cake and candy. At last year's party, they also enjoyed eating the edible decorations from the tree! At the end of the party, the group picked up the tree and tossed it out into the snow.

Christmas Eve is a day of many legends and traditions. Farmers bring their tools inside so the wandering shoemaker from Jerusalem does not sit on them and bewitch them. Family and friends dip pieces of bread into the broth from boiling the ham. And then there's the *tomte*, the Christmas gnome! Tradition says the tomte lives under the floorboards of the house. From there, he keeps the family and children safe. In homes with small children, someone dresses up like *jultomte* — another name for Santa Claus. He shows up on the doorstep with a sack of presents slung over his back.

In the early hours of Christmas Day, a candlelit church service called *julotta* is held. In some places people still race home in wagons or sleds. In rural areas, the winner is assured of a good harvest.

Christmas dinner at grandfather Bergland's house.

This year, Isabel and her mother spend Christmas at her grandfather's home in Norrköping. Christmas dinner is a smörgåsbord of traditional dishes: ham, pickled pig's feet, and *lutfisk*. Lutfisk is a fish that is dried in a way that was used before there were refrigerators. After it is dried, the fish is boiled. Next year she will have Christmas with her grandmother on her father's side. Both families treasure the time they spend with Isabel.

Christmas night passes quietly. Isabel falls asleep filled with the joy of the day and hope for the new year.

FOR YOUR INFORMATION: Sweden

Official name: Konungariket Sverige   Kingdom of Sweden
                    [KONE-un-yah-rree-ket   seh-VAH-rree-yeh]

Capital: Stockholm

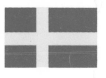

Bicycle lanes make for pleasant commuting into Stockholm.

History

Early Scandinavian History

The civilization of Sweden began sometime between 7000 and 5000 B.C. This is when the last of the glaciers melted. Hunters and farmers moved onto the once ice-covered land. By 3000 B.C., they had begun settlements and were growing crops.

Ancient tribes in the land that is now Sweden were quite warlike and traveled far and wide. Stone monuments to leaders and military campaigns prove that the Swedish Vikings traveled through Russia. These monuments, called runestones, date back to 1000 A.D.

Sweden's history is closely tied to the other Scandinavian countries — Norway, Denmark, Finland, and Iceland. At times the countries were united, but not always in a friendly way. Their history is joined together from around 1150 A.D., when Sweden ruled Finland. Around 1300, Norway and Sweden were united. Denmark ruled Sweden and Norway from around 1400 till 1523, when King Gustav tore Sweden away from Denmark. In 1814, Norway broke away from Denmark, and Sweden and Norway were reunited. That union lasted till 1905.

Sweden's Development as a Nation

By 1200 Sweden was trading with German cities, and Stockholm was becoming a center of power. In the late 1400s a form of Parliament existed. It represented four groups: nobles, clergy, business people, and peasants. In 1523, Sweden had its first King — Gustav Eriksson Vasa. Sweden and its King had great power. Sweden carried on trade — and wars — with other European countries.

48

In 1719 a new constitution gave more power to Sweden's Parliament. Two parties dominated the government. One was made up of business people, and the other represented the people in general. In 1772 a revolt resulted in royal rule once again till 1792, when the King was assassinated. A new constitution came into being in 1809. It set up a balance of power between King and Parliament. In 1814, after war with Russia, Sweden decided not to fight in any more wars and declared itself a neutral state.

In the 19th century, Sweden's economy began to change. It had been based on farming, and now it was becoming industrial. The population grew quickly, and from 1860 to 1914 more than a million people left the country. Most went to North America. Industry replaced farming as a way to earn a living. The Swedes who stayed moved from the countryside to the cities. The Industrial Revolution came later to Sweden than to the rest of Europe because Sweden lacked the coal to power heavy industry. Instead, Sweden pioneered new machines. Swedish inventors also developed the first cream separator and milking machine. They invented one of the first telephones, beginning an industry that thrives in Sweden today.

In the mid 1800s, Alfred Nobel made a fortune as the inventor of dynamite. Dynamite became a key factor in the growth of the mining and construction industries. His will set up the Nobel Prizes. These prizes honor international writers, scientists, and humanitarians.

Sweden in the 20th Century

By 1900, Sweden had become a modern industrialized society. Its government was becoming more and more liberal. It developed policies that would lead to Sweden's current social programs. These programs ensure economic and social security to all its citizens.

Sweden stayed neutral through both World Wars. However, neutrality came at a high price in World War II. In order to remain neutral and unoccupied, Sweden allowed German troops and equipment to cross the country and invade Norway. Since World War II, Sweden has built up its defense system. Sweden thus intends that its neutrality will never again contribute to the harm of another country's people.

A Hero of World War II

Though his government was neutral, a Swede — Raoul Wallenberg — was one of the war's great heroes. Months before the end of the war, the U.S. asked Wallenberg to do what he could to rescue Jews in the German-occupied city of Budapest, Hungary. In Budapest, as in all of Europe, Nazi Germany's goal was to remove Jews from their homes to camps, where they were murdered.

Wallenberg saved thousands of Jews by giving them papers that made them instant Swedish citizens. This put them under Swedish protection. And because Sweden was neutral, the Nazis could not harm its citizens, no matter where they were. Survivors tell how Wallenberg pulled some of them from trains bound for the death camps, thrusting papers into their hands as he bluffed his way past the German guards.

49

The day the Soviets took Budapest from the Nazis, Wallenberg presented himself to the Soviet military leaders. He wished to offer his services as a representative of Sweden. The Soviets arrested him, and he was never seen again outside a Soviet prison. The Soviet Union has never explained why Wallenberg was arrested.

For the next several decades, prisoners who escaped from the Soviet Union would relay messages from Wallenberg. The United States, Sweden, and Israel tried to find him and free him. But their efforts were too little and probably too late. In recent years, stories of him have ceased. After many years of denying he had ever been there, the Soviets now say he had died in prison.

In 1981, U.S. Representative Tom Lantos of California introduced a bill that made Raoul Wallenberg an honorary U.S. citizen. In 1944, with the help of Wallenberg, the Hungarian-born Lantos had escaped the Nazi roundup of Jews. The U.S. has finally honored Wallenberg for his heroism — 36 years after his arrest. Also, now that Wallenberg was officially a U.S. citizen, the government could ask the U.S.S.R. formally about his condition. Canada and Israel have also made Wallenberg an honorary citizen of their countries. And Sweden has finally honored him, too — with a special postage stamp.

Sweden Today: A Land of Immigrants

Only a hundred years ago, Sweden was a poor country. Its wealth was concentrated in the hands of few people. Today the economy of Sweden provides work and a living for many people. Many people migrate there in search of jobs and religious and political freedom. Since 1945, immigrants and their children have added 800,000 to the population of Sweden. One in ten Swedes is either an immigrant or a child of one. Half of these new Swedes come from Finland. Since the mid 1960s however, many have come from Yugoslavia, Greece, Turkey, and other European countries, and from Latin America.

Population and Ethnic Groups

Sweden's Many Cultures

About 83% of Sweden's 8,500,000 people live in the cities. Most Swedes are descended from the early Viking settlers. These settlers first came to Sweden when the glaciers melted in 7000–5000 B.C. They were from two main tribes, the Goths and the Svear. Today, Sweden has welcomed people whose native cultures and languages are not Swedish. The educational and social systems have expanded their services to meet the needs of recent immigrants. Children receive special teaching from speakers of their native language. Workers can spend up to 240 hours learning Swedish at full pay.

The Sami

Sweden also has a large native minority population. It lives to the north in the region known as Lappland. Lappland stretches across the top of Norway, Sweden, Finland, and into the Soviet Union. Its latitude is about the same as Alaska's. The Lapps speak 50 versions of a language that is related to Finnish. The name *Lapp* is from the Finnish. Its meaning is unknown. Most Swedish Lapps speak their native language and Swedish. About 15,000 of the 40,000 Lapps live in Sweden. They refer to themselves as *Sami.*

Sami (Lapplander) herders and their reindeer in the far north.

Their heavy wool clothing shows the embroidery and overall style for which the Sami are known.

Some scholars believe that the Sami moved into the far north from Asia around 500 B.C. on the trail of reindeer. Others date their migration several thousand years earlier. At first, the Sami followed the reindeer, hunting and trapping. Wild reindeer herds migrate as the seasons change, returning to the same grazing lands. It was natural for the Sami to follow one herd. Gradually, Sami tribes became less nomadic.

Most Sami live in Lappland, but more and more come south to work. Most Sami fish, mine, and farm cattle and sheep. About 20% still make their living following reindeer herds. Today only breeders and younger men follow and supervise the herd. They drive it from one grazing ground to another.

The reindeer is the only domesticated animal in the world that can feed itself on the meager vegetation beyond the Arctic Circle. Herders driving the reindeer live in a teepee or hut called a *kåta*. They get around by snowmobile. Traditionally, specially tamed reindeer, called *härkor*, carried supplies or pulled sleds, or *akja*. The reindeer were roped together forming a caravan called a *rajd*. The Sami also invented skis as a way of getting around. The word *ski* comes from *Skridfinrna*, an old Scandinavian name for Lappland. *Skrid* means to slide.

The village of Jukkasjärvi is a kind of headquarters for the Sami. It has a modern school where Sami children learn in their own language as well as Swedish. It also has a home for aged Sami and a church built in 1726. The Sami are not a simple people. They understand their rights, and they are organized to protect their heritage. They are the only ones who can herd reindeer. They also have special grazing, hunting, and fishing rights. The government gives them financial help to preserve their language and culture.

Lappland has become something of a tourist center. It attracts visitors by train and plane from Stockholm. The Sami have begun to produce handicrafts for the growing tourist trade. Their materials include the horns and skin of reindeer.

The Sami are proud of their heritage and traditions. Though smaller than most Swedes, they are strong and independent. The Sami population varies in lifestyle and dialect, costume, and present day religion. Yet they feel ties to other Sami across Lappland as well as to Sweden. In World War II, they helped Norwegians and others fleeing from the Nazis to escape from Norway through the Swedish mountains. They value their culture and way of life very strongly. This and the Swedish government's support of their efforts assure that their identity will survive.

Language

Swedish is the national language of Sweden. In the schools, all children are taught to read and write in both Swedish and English. The many immigrants to Sweden are also taught in their native language, however. The Sami in the north speak varieties of a language believed to come from Finnish.

Religion

Most Swedes belong to the Lutheran State Church. Most do not attend church services, however, or concern themselves with church matters. Sweden observes most Christian holidays in ways that combine traditional Swedish customs with biblical beliefs. Most of the Sami are Christian, but many remember the old religious ways.

Education

All children between seven and sixteen must go to school. For the first six years, all students take the same courses. Generally the class has just one teacher who teaches all subjects. From 7th grade on, subjects are taught by specialized teachers. All children study English from 3rd or 4th grade through 9th grade. Starting in 7th grade, children may choose to study a third language — French, German, or home language for immigrant children. Or they may take another elective that the school offers. All children must take courses in technology, home economics, and child care. In the later years of required school, students must receive 6-10 weeks of practical work experience outside school.

Children do not get grades for their work until 8th grade. Teachers report on their progress in conferences with the parents. In 8th and 9th grades students are graded on a scale of 1-5, with five being the highest. There are no final exams.

Over 90% of all students continue their education after they complete their required courses. The next program offers 2-4 years of study in one of 25 categories. It must include English and Swedish language studies to qualify the student for college. Students get grades at the end of each term, but they don't take final exams.

College is free in Sweden, and the government may pay students' living expenses. However, space is limited, and not everyone who qualifies can get in.

Sports

International stars like Björn Borg and Ingemar Stenmark have made Sweden famous in the sports world. Because of them, many young Swedes are interested in tennis and Alpine skiiing. For most of sports-minded Sweden, soccer is the most popular game. Soccer is played by people of all ages and abilities. Ice hockey is Sweden's favorite winter team sport. Some Swedish hockey players go on to play professionally in Canada and the U.S.

Less competitive, more solitary sports include jogging, cross-country and downhill skiing, hiking, and gymnastics. Swimming, bicycling, and ice skating are also popular. Swedes also feel very much at home in the woods. *Allemansrätten*, the right of access, allows people to pass freely through forests or across open land, to pick mushrooms or berries, and even to swim or dock a boat. The only condition is that they do not litter or invade the owner's privacy.

The government pays for many athletic programs. In this way, everyone can take part. Many programs help older people and people with disabilities keep fit and enjoy life more. Most large companies have a gymnasium or sports club for employees and their families.

The Arts

The Swedish government encourages all people to develop their talents and to paticipate in the arts. The government pays for theaters and other arts programs all over the country. It also pays Stockholm dance and theater groups to take their programs to areas in the north. In Stockholm, right next to the royal palace, is a theater that was built in 1766. Here plays from the 17th and 18th centuries are performed as they were when they were first written.

Skansen, an open air folk museum, has been in Stockholm since 1891. Skansen is equipped and decorated just as it was then. Here craftspeople make iron and wood products, glass, and lace — and they dress — just as folk artists did in the past. The museum is sometimes called a museum of folk life. It is more than just a tourist attraction. It is a way of preserving knowledge and skills from the past by using them today. Every New Year's Eve since the turn of the century, Stockholmers gather at Skansen. There they hear a reading of Alfred Lord Tennyson's poem "Ring Out the Old, Ring in the New." Museums like Skansen exist all over Europe. They are beginning to appear in the U.S. and Canada.

Many writers and artists from Sweden are well known in North America. Many children here have read the *Pippi Longstocking* books by Astrid Lindgren. Ms. Lindgren has written over eighty children's books which have been translated into over forty languages. Carl Larsson's books about his farm and his children are also available here. They have beautiful drawings from the beginning of the century of life in rural Sweden. Also, Larsson's murals appear on many public buildings in Sweden.

Sweden is a neutral country. But its position of trust among disputing nations does not lessen its awareness of world tensions. This underground parking lot in Stockholm doubles as an air-raid shelter. It is stocked with food and other necessities.

Government

Sweden is a constitutional monarchy. The *Riksdagen,* or Parliament, has 349 members in one chamber. As the supreme legislative body, Parliament must approve the appointment of the Prime Minister. The King is head of the state. Because of constitutional reforms in 1980, however, his responsibilities are only ceremonial.

The Swedish government provides economic, educational, medical, and social services for all its people. For example, in remote northern areas the population is small and the distances are great. Therefore, the cost of many services in these areas is expensive. The government picks up some of the cost of these services. This evens out the cost of living in different parts of the country. Sweden also gives a lot of its money and products to poor and insecure nations.

54

When Alfred Nobel made his will laying out the conditions for the Nobel Prizes, Sweden and Norway were jointly governed. The will stated that the Nobel Peace Prize would be given by a Norwegian committee elected by their Parliament. Within a few years, Sweden and Norway were no longer united, but the prize winners are still chosen by the Norwegians. In 1973, the Peace Prize was awarded to Henry Kissinger of the U.S. and Le Duc Tho of North Vietnam. They had negotiated a temporary cease-fire in the midst of the Vietnam War. Many Swedes were outraged and called it the "Nobel War Prize." Now the Swedish and Norwegian governments agree to a rule. The Peace Prize will be given only to those who do not use force as a general way of solving problems. The Peace Prize is still controversial, however. And it probably will be as long as government officials are awarded the prize.

Land

Sweden, the fourth largest country in Europe, is slightly larger than California. It is nearly 1000 miles (1600 km) long and about 300 miles (500 km) wide. More than half the land is covered with coniferous forests. It is bordered by Norway on the west, Finland to the northeast, the Baltic Sea and the Gulf of Bothnia to the east, and, across a narrow body of water called the Kattegat, Denmark to the south. Just across the Baltic from Sweden are the U.S.S.R., Poland, and East and West Germany. A mountain range left behind by a glacier makes up the northern Swedish-Norwegian border. The north is also marked by coniferous forests and strong-running rivers. The south is more open, with deciduous trees and farmland.

Frozen seas are cleared away by ice-breakers in the Gulf of Bothnia.

Climate

Because Sweden is nearly 1 000 miles (1 600 km) from north to south, the climate varies from one area to another. In February, for instance, the average temperature in Kiruna, in the north, is 9°F (-12.9°C). In Malmö, in the south, it is 31°F (-0.79°C). Sweden's latitude is the same as Alaska's, but its general climate is mild because of the warm Atlantic Gulf Stream. From December through March northern Sweden is covered with snow. In the south, the amount of snow varies each year, as it does in the snowy regions of the United States and southern Canada. Northern Sweden is sometimes called the Land of the Midnight Sun. Here, north of the Arctic Circle, you can see the sun 24 hours a day for several weeks in the summer.

In the winter, the sun is gone for months, although there is a little light around noon. Even in the more southern regions, the days are much longer in summer than in winter. On December 21 in Stockholm, the sun rises at 9:00 a.m. and sets before 3:00 p.m. On June 21st, it rises at 2:30 a.m. and sets after 9:00 p.m.

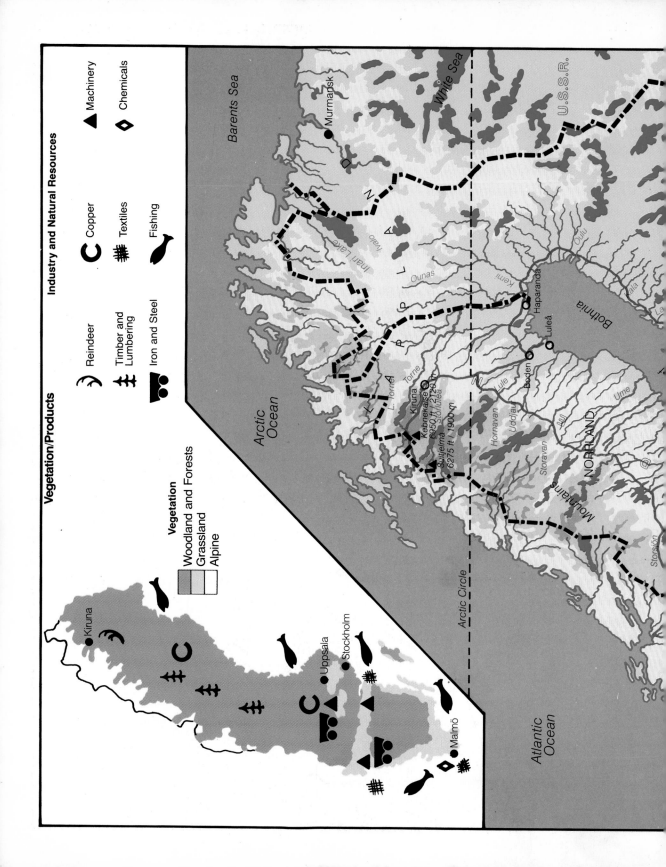

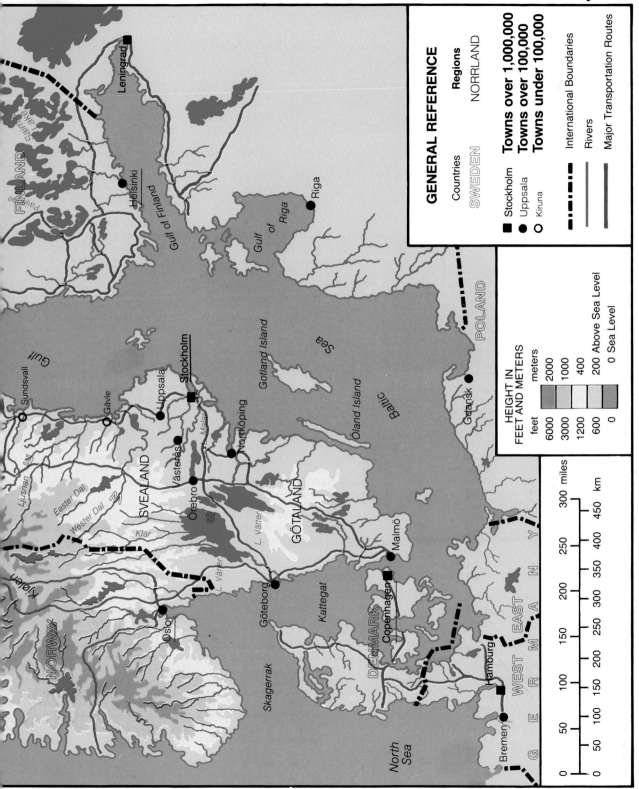

GENERAL REFERENCE

Countries	Regions
SWEDEN	NORRLAND

Towns over 1,000,000
Towns over 100,000
Towns under 100,000

■ Stockholm   International Boundaries
● Uppsala   Rivers
○ Kiruna   Major Transportation Routes

HEIGHT IN
FEET AND METERS

feet	meters
6000	2000
3000	1000
1200	400
600	200 Above Sea Level
0	0 Sea Level

FINLAND
Saimaa Lake
Leningrad
Helsinki
Gulf of Finland
Gulf of Riga
Riga
POLAND
Gdansk
Gulf
Sundsvall
Gävle
Uppsala
Stockholm
Västerås
Örebro
Norrköping
Gotland Island
Baltic Sea
Öland Island
SVEALAND
GÖTALAND
Easter Dal
Wester Dal
Klar
Ljusnan
Mälar
L. Vätter
L. Väner
NORWAY
Kjölen
Oslo
Göteborg
Kattegat
Skagerrak
DENMARK
Copenhagen
Malmö
North Sea
Hamburg
Bremen
WEST EAST
GERMANY

miles	km
0	0
50	50
100	150
150	200
200	250
250	300
300	350
	400
	450

Stockholm: A city of bridges, islands, and waterfronts.

Stockholm

Stockholm became the capital of Sweden in 1436. Today it has 1.5 million people. Sometimes called the Venice of the north, Stockholm consists of 14 islands in Lake Malar. It is a city of bridges and waterfronts. All waters in the city are fit for swimming. The city plants trout and salmon in the lake waters.

Twenty-four thousand islands form a large group called the Stockholm Archipelago. The inner islands are Stockholm itself. Some islands are suburbs. They fan out 12 miles (19 km) in all directions. They are connected by bridge or ferry to the city. Others form what is known as Summer Stockholm, thousands of islands with summer homes on the seaward side of the city. In the past, hundreds of small boats came daily to sell fish in Stockholm. Today, like any bus or subway system, "bus boats" take commuters and tourists around the islands.

Currency

The *krona* and *öre* are the basic Swedish currency. One krona = 100 öre.

Natural Resources

Since the 18th century, Swedes have done a lot to help save the environment. Even before World War I, Sweden had six national parks. Today, there are nearly 1500 national parks and protected wildlife areas. In addition to iron ore, Sweden's main natural resources are its immense forests and hydroelectric power. Many forests and lakes have been affected by acid rain. Fumes from cars have made some wild berries and mushrooms unfit for eating. Swedes have designed equipment at thermal power plants to reduce emissions that cause acid rains. And because air and water pollution does not stop at national boundaries, Sweden is active in the international movement to keep the Baltic Sea clean.

Industry and Agriculture

In Norrland, the northern lake and mountain region, the forests are carefully managed. These forests form one of the largest timber industries in the world. Timber and the products made from it, such as paper, pulp, and sawn wood, are not the only products in the region. An industry also produces machinery *for* the timber industry. The iron ore, copper, and other minerals make Norrland one of Europe's richest mining areas. This area and Lappland make up half of Sweden's territory. Yet only 17% of the population lives there.

Only 8% of Sweden's land is cultivated. However, that is enough to make Sweden nearly self-sufficient in agricultural products. The plains of Skåne, Sweden's most southern province, produce sugar beets, wheat, barley, and livestock. The livestock produce butter, cheese, milk, and meat.

In 1986, 100,000 of the 250,000–300,000 Swedish Sami reindeer herds ate food contaminated by the Chernobyl nuclear accident in the Soviet Ukraine. At first, it seemed nearly half the reindeer in Sweden would have to be destroyed. This seemed the only way to prevent spread of the radiation to humans and animals that ate the meat. Instead the Swedish government bought some of the meat to feed to animals on mink and fox farms. The mink and fox are not part of the human food chain. The expensive coats made from their fur would not be affected. This action saved some income for the Sami herders. However, the accident was still very damaging because so many reindeer had to be killed, and the herd sizes were reduced. Also, contaminated animals could not be allowed to reproduce. Therefore, the herds could not grow as quickly as before.

The industrial areas in south and central Sweden produce cars, ball bearings, and electrical equipment.   Sweden is also known for its creative designing.

Swedish textiles, crystal, and furniture are known all over the world for their beauty and quality. In the John F. Kennedy Center in Washington, D.C., hang chandeliers that are 13 feet long (4 m), each weighing 13 tons. These chandeliers, from the Orrefors Glass Company of Sweden, are a product of Swedish industry and design.

About 70% of Sweden's trade is with Western European countries. About 11% of its exports go to the U.S., which supplies about 8% of its imports. Canada accounts for 1.3% of its exports and .6% of its imports. Its main exports are wood products and iron ore, machinery, electrical products, and transportation equipment.

Sweden has 12 nuclear reactors, but it will phase them out by 2010 as the result of a public vote in 1980. Also, Sweden no longer mines uranium or exports reactors. Clearly, Sweden is moving away from nuclear-based industry. Also, the Chernobyl accident has made the Swedes more determined to reduce their dependence on nuclear power. The Chernobyl accident spread radioactive iodine and cesium over Sweden's fields, forests, and lakes.

Swedish Immigrants in North America

One hundred years ago, Sweden was well on its way to becoming the poorest country in Europe. The wealth was concentrated in the hands of a few, and the country could not support its people. During these years about a million Swedes left their country. Most of them came as farmers to the midwestern U.S. Some stopped at the Canadian port cities of Halifax, Québec, and Montréal. But most followed the St. Lawrence Seaway around the Great Lakes till they reached Minnesota. Some settled there, and others settled in western Wisconsin, the Dakotas, and, in Canada, in Manitoba, Saskatchewan, and Alberta. From these states and provinces, many Swedes migrated further west, to Oregon, Washington, and British Columbia. There, they worked in the lumber industry. Descendants of the early immigrants still live in these areas. Many of them keep their ties to the old country. They form organizations to celebrate and keep alive the ways of their ancestors. One such organization is the Swedish Vasa Order of America. On St. Lucia's Day, daughters of Swedish descent rise early to celebrate the ancient Swedish holiday, much as their cousins are doing in Sweden.

Glossary of Swedish Terms

akja (AH-kyah) . . . . sled (Sami)
allemansrätten
(AH-leh-mahns-rreh-ten) . . everyone's right to free access to land and water
häkor (HEH-korr) . . . . reindeer trained to carry supplies or pull sleds (Sami)
julotta (YULE-loh-tah) . . . . a special early service on Christmas morning
kåta (KOH-tah) . . . . a Sami teepee or hut
kömer (KUH-merr) . . . . market (Sami)
lutfisk (LUTE-fisk) . . . . a fish dried and boiled; usually a Christmas meal
pannbiff (PAHN-beef) . . . . a meat dish, like a hamburger
pepparkakor
(PEH-parr-kah-korr) . . . . . gingersnap cookies
rajd (RRIDE) . . . . a caravan of reindeer (Sami)

saltlakrits
  (SAHLT-lak-riss) . . . . a licorice candy with a salty taste
Sami (SAW-mee) . . . . Lapp people or Lappish language
sita (SEE-tah)
  (plural *sitor*) . . . . a group of 2–4 Sami families, usually built around
                                a herd of reindeer
skrid (SKRREED) . . . . to slide (Sami; *Skrida* in Swedish)
Skridfinrna
  (skrreed-FEEN-rr-nah) . . . . old Scandinavian name for Lappland
smörgåsbord
  (SMERR-gose-boorrd) . . . a variety of tasty foods served buffet style
tomte (TOHM-teh) . . . . a gnome; Santa Claus is also called *jultomte*

More Books About Sweden

Here are more books about Sweden. If you are interested in them, check your library. Many of them may be helpful in doing research for the "Things to Do" projects that follow.

Christmas in Noisy Village. Lindgren (Penguin)
Elvis and His Secret. Gripe (Dell)
A Farm. Larsson (Putnam)
A House. Larsson (Putnam)
Kirsten Learns a Lesson: A School Story. Shaw (Pleasant Company)
Kirsten's Surprise: A Christmas Story. Shaw (Pleasant Company)
Meet Kirsten: An American Girl. Shaw (Pleasant Company)
Pippi Longstocking. Lindgren (Viking)
Swedes In America. Hillbrand (Greenhaven Press)
Tomten. Lindgren (Putnam)

Things to Do — Research Projects

Governments and economies change quickly. In the mid 1970s, for example, Sweden relied strongly on nuclear power and was building and expanding its nuclear power plants. Within 10 years, however, Swedes had passed a law calling for an end to nuclear power by the year 2010. A nuclear accident in neighboring U.S.S.R. had affected Swedish vegetation and animal life. In Sweden, the tide was clearly shifting.

As you read about Sweden, or any country, keep in mind the importance of having current information. Some of the research projects that follow need accurate, up-to-date information. That is why current newspapers and magazines are useful sources of information. Two publications your library may have will tell you about recent magazine and newspaper articles on many topics:

Readers' Guide to Periodical Literature
Children's Magazine Guide

1. Compare the immigration policies of your country with Sweden's. What are the restrictions? What rights would you have as a refugee from another country? Which country would make you feel welcome as an ethnic minority?

2. Write a short report about a resource or industry important to Sweden's economy. Be sure your information is current, at least within the last year.

3. Imagine your parents decided to move to Sweden. Investigate further into Sweden and pick an area in which you'd like to live. Give your reasons.

4. Look up Sweden in the *Readers' Guide to Periodical Literature* or the *Children's Magazine Guide*. Find articles that have been written recently, and report to classmates about what has been happening in the last few months.

5. Pick a Swedish holiday that your country also celebrates. How do the two celebrations resemble each other?

More Things to Do — Activities

These projects are designed to encourage you to think more about Sweden. They offer ideas for interesting group or individual projects that you can do at school or at home.

1. How far is Stockholm from where you live? Using maps, travel guides, travel agents, or any other resources you know of, find out how you could get there and how long it would take.

2. In Sweden it is illegal for adults to physically or psychologically harm a child. All Swedish children know this law and the phone number to call if they have been abused. Is there a number or an agency you could call if you had to?

3. On New Year's Eve, people in Stockholm gather to hear a reading of "Ring Out the Old, Ring in the New," a poem by the English poet Tennyson. Those who can't attend listen to the reading on the radio. Find a copy of the poem in your library and read it to your friends to celebrate the New Year.

4. Here is a recipe for a Swedish dessert called baked apples in cream. You will need:

6 large apples	4 teaspoons (20 ml) cinnamon
⅓ cup (85 ml) sugar	¼ cup (62.5 ml) crushed ginger cookies
6 tablespoons (90 ml) butter	½ cup (125 ml) whipping cream

Wash and peel the apples. Cut out the cores. Mix cinnamon and sugar together. Melt the butter. Roll the apples in the butter, and then in the cinnamon and sugar. Stand the apples upright in a shallow pan. Fill the hollow centers with the remaining cinnamon and sugar. Top the centers with the remaining butter. Bake at 350°F (180°C) for 20 minutes. Pour the cream over and around the apples. Bake for 30 more minutes until the apples are tender but not mushy.

5. How does your life compare with Isabel's? Write an imaginary letter to her. Explain the ways in which you are the same or different.

6. If you would like a pen pal in Sweden, write to these people: International Pen Friends
P.O. Box 290065
Brooklyn, NY 11229-000

Be sure to tell them what country you want your pen pal to be from. Also include your full name and address.

Index

Bjener, Tamiko.
    Sweden / photography by Tamiko Bjener
; edited by MaryLee Knowlton & Mark J.
Sachner. -- Milwaukee : G. Stevens
Pub., 1987.
    63 p. : col. ill. ; 24 cm. --
(Children of the world)
    Bibliography: p. 61.
                    x.
            and photographs present
            by following eleven-
year-old Isabel, child of divorced
parents, as she moves between her two
families.
    ISBN 1-55532-189-5